Frances

Frances

An adaptation of the Gospel of Luke

Rev. Dr. Jeff Hood

WIPF & STOCK · Eugene, Oregon

FRANCES
An Adaptation of the Gospel of Luke

Copyright © 2016 Jeff Hood. All rights reserved. Except for brief quotations in critical publications or reviews, no part of this book may be reproduced in any manner without prior written permission from the publisher. Write: Permissions, Wipf and Stock Publishers, 199 W. 8th Ave., Suite 3, Eugene, OR 97401.

Wipf & Stock
An Imprint of Wipf and Stock Publishers
199 W. 8th Ave., Suite 3
Eugene, OR 97401

www.wipfandstock.com

PAPERBACK ISBN: 978-1-5326-1244-2
HARDCOVER ISBN: 978-1-5326-1246-6

Manufactured in the U.S.A.   NOVEMBER 29, 2016

Cover Painting: "The Jesus with Many Feet" by Emily Hood

To All the Women Who Have Been Jesus to Me

1.

I tried to write it all down as it came to me. The events were so magical and beautiful. In addition to my own thoughts, I interacted with the accounts of others to prepare this account. I wrote all of this for my children. I want them to know the truth.

There once was a good pastor named Elizabeth. God was pleased with Elizabeth and her husband Ed. The couple had no children. Elizabeth was too old.

One day, Elizabeth was preparing the elements for communion and an angel of God appeared to her. The doors of her church slammed shut. When Elizabeth saw the angel, she fell down terrified and was unable to speak. The angel said, "Do not be afraid. You are going to carry a son and his name will be John. Everyone will rejoice at his birth. John will be filled with the Holy Spirit and great in the eyes of both God and humanity. Despite the pressures of the culture, you must make sure that he never succumbs to materialism. With tremendous prophetic power, John will turn many hearts toward truth and prepare people to meet the incarnation of God." Elizabeth said, "How can I know this is true? I am old and so is my husband." The angel replied, "I am Gabriel. I stand in the presence of God and was sent directly to you. But now, because you did not believe me, you will be unable to speak until the birth of John."

Meanwhile, people couldn't figure out why the doors were shut and stood outside waiting to get into the sanctuary for service. When Elizabeth came out, her clothes were glowing and she was unable to speak. Ed couldn't figure out what was happening. On a tablet, Elizabeth wrote it all down and Ed read it aloud. In tremendous gratitude, Elizabeth went back into the sanctuary and served communion to the church.

Elizabeth conceived a child and stayed at home throughout the pregnancy.

In the sixth month of Elizabeth's pregnancy, Gabriel went to a virgin named Mary. The angel said to her, "Do not be afraid. Mary, you are favored by God. You will conceive a daughter in your womb and name her Frances. She will be great and will be called the Daughter of God. She will reign over all nature and there will be no end to her reign." Mary questioned Gabriel, "How can this be? I am a virgin." The angel replied, "The Holy Spirit will come into you. The child will be the Daughter of God. And now, your relative Elizabeth has conceived a son in her old age. She is in her sixth month. Nothing is impossible for God." Mary declared, "I am here God. Let it be according to your word." Then the angel departed.

Mary left immediately. Traveling a great distance to the home of her cousin, Mary and Elizabeth embraced when they saw each other. The child in Elizabeth's womb jumped up and down in excitement. Elizabeth shouted out, "Blessed are you and the fruit of your womb. God is with you."

And Mary responded, "My soul rejoices in God. My spirit sings within me. God is my savior. God has looked with favor on me. All generations will call me blessed. God has looked upon me and placed a child within me. The mercy of God extends from generation to generation. God has scattered the proud and lifted up the humble. God lifts the lowly. God sends the rich away empty and fills the hungry with food. God has helped all people and will not leave the people of this earth." Mary stayed with Elizabeth for three months and then returned home.

Elizabeth gave birth and bore a son. The entire community rejoiced with her. On the eighth day, the time came to circumcise the child and the gathered assumed his name would be Ed after his dad. Speaking ofr the first time in months, Elizabeth responded strongly, "His name is John!" They said to her, "none of your relatives have that name." Everyone motioned to his dad to clear things up. Ed declared, "His name is John." And everyone was amazed. Immediately, the tongue of Elizabeth began to praise God. Fear came over all their neighbors, and the story became known throughout Texas. All who heard the beautiful words pondered them and said, "What will this child become?" The hand of God was upon him.

Elizabeth was filled with the Holy Spirit and started to prophesy: "How great is our God? With love and mercy God has looked upon us. A mighty savior has been raised. God spoke through the prophets and saved us. The mercies of God are new every day. We are rescued from our enemies. We serve God without fear all of our days. And you, my dear John, will be called the prophet of the Daughter of God. You will go before our savior and prepare her ways. You will give knowledge of salvation to all her people by the forgiveness of sins. Dawn will break through and shine through you. All who sit in darkness will see a great light. The shadow of death will be no more. She will guide our feet into the way of peace." The child grew and became strong in spirit, and he was in the wilderness until the day he appeared publicly.

2.

In those days an executive order went out from the President that all must be registered in a census. The Governor of Texas consented to this registration. All went to their towns to participate in the census. Since he was descended from a family in West Texas, Joseph had to return to Lubbock. He went to be registered with Mary, who was pregnant. While they were there, the time came for Mary to give birth. And she gave birth to her firstborn daughter and wrapped her in rags, and laid her on an old mattress behind a dumpster, because the hospital wouldn't take their insurance.

In that region there were drillers in the desert, keeping watch over their rigs by night. Then the angel of God stood before them, and the glory of God shown all around them, and they were terrified. But the angel said to them, "Do not be afraid. I bring you the most incredible news you have ever heard. The Daughter of God who is the Messiah was born in Lubbock tonight. You will find the child wrapped in rags and lying on an old mattress behind a dumpster." And suddenly the entire sky was filled with a multitude of angels and everything else, praising God and saying, "Glory to God in the highest, and on earth peace among those who God favors!"

When the angels left, the drillers said to each other, "Let's go to Lubbock!" Quickly, the drillers went to exactly the right dumpster and found Mary, Joseph and the child lying in the manger. Everyone was amazed at the story the drillers told, but Mary remained silent and treasured them in her heart. The drillers returned to their rigs praising God for all they had seen and heard.

Mary called the child Frances, the name that the angel told her.

The time came for the child to be baptized at a local church in Fort Worth. During the ceremony, there was a priest named Simeon. Many years prior, God told Simeon that he would not die until he saw the Messiah. Guided by the Spirit, Simeon held the child up at the moment of baptism and proclaimed, "I can die now. In this beautiful girl, I have seen your salvation for all people. Frances will save our enemies and our friends."
Joseph and Mary were blown away by what was happening. Simeon baptized the child and said, "This child will save us all. Frances will pierce our very hearts and souls."

There was a prophet named Anna. She was very old and stayed at church in prayer all the time. When she saw Frances, Anna praised God and told everyone that she had met the redemption that the world was waiting on.

Once they finished the baptism in Fort Worth, the family returned to their hometown of Waco. Frances grew in strength and wisdom. The favor of God was upon her.

Now every year her parents returned to Fort Worth for a religious festival called Passover. When Frances was twelve years old, the family went to the festival as usual. When the festival was over and they started to return, Frances stayed behind in Fort Worth, but her parents did not know it. The family got all the way back to Waco before they realized that Frances was not in the car that they thought she was in. Immediately, the family returned back to Fort Worth. After a considerable amount of time, the family found Frances teaching and interacting with religious leaders in a church. Everyone was amazed at the knowledge of Frances. When Mary saw her, she demanded, "Why have you treated us like this? We have looked all over the city for you." She replied, "Why are you looking for me? Did you not know that I would be teaching about God?" But the family did not understand what Frances was talking about. Then she left to travel back to Waco with them. Mary continued to ponder everything in her heart.

Throughout the years, Frances only increased in divine and human favor.

3.

Later, the word of God came to John son of Elizabeth and Ed in the desert. He went into the region around Waco, proclaiming a baptism of repentance for the forgiveness of sins, as it was prophesied in the words of Isaiah, "The voice of the one crying out in the desert, 'Prepare the way of God! Make his paths straight. Every valley shall be filled. Every mountain and hill will be made low. The crooked shall be made straight. The rough ways will be made smooth. All flesh will see the salvation of God.'"

John said to the crowds who came out to be baptized, "You brood of vipers! Who warned you to flee from what is coming? Bear fruit worthy of repentance. Do not just say that you are an American. Who cares? Every tree that does not bear fruit will be thrown out."

The crowds asked him, "What are we supposed to do?" In reply, John said, "Share your food and clothes with the poor." Even the police and army came to be baptized, asking, "What should we do?" He said to them, "Put down your weapons and don't use them ever again." Politicians asked him, "What should we do?" John replied, "Stop using the people for your gain!"

Everyone thought that John was the Messiah. Sensing their thoughts, John said, "I baptize you with water, but there is one coming that is much greater than I. I am not worthy to untie her shoes. She will baptize you with the Holy Spirit and fire. She is going to really clean things up."

John continued to proclaim the good news to people. Unfortunately, the Governor got tired of John speaking of the injustices of his administration and tossed him in prison.

Before John was put in prison, Frances had also been baptized. During the baptism, the heavens opened up and the Spirit descended upon her in the form of a dove. A beautiful voice came from heaven and declared, "You are my beloved Daughter. Save them."

Frances was about thirty years old when she started her work. Unfortunately, Frances knew little about where she came from.

4.

The Spirit led Frances into the wilderness. For forty days and nights, Frances was tempted by all manners of evil. Eating nothing, Frances quickly became famished. Evil looked her in the face and said, "If you are the Daughter of God, make some food appear." Frances replied, "We do not live by food alone." Then evil led her up and showed her all the nations on the planet. Evil said to her, "If you will worship me, I will give you all of this." Frances replied, "I worship God alone." Evil tried again and took her to the top of the State Capitol of Texas and said, "If you are the Daughter of God, throw your self down and command the angels to catch you." Frances replied, "We are not to put God to the test." When every test was complete, evil departed and waited for another opportunity to snag Frances.

Filled with the power of the Spirit, Frances was taken back to Fort Worth and started to teach in every religious space she could find. The media throughout the region talked about her. Lives started to be miraculously changed through Frances' teachings.

When Frances arrived at her home of Waco, she went to church. Standing in the pulpit, Frances read the words of Isaiah, "The Spirit of God is within me. God has appointed me to proclaim good news to the poor. I have been sent to set the captives free. The blind will receive sight. The oppressed will be set free. I am here to proclaim the year of God's favor." Everyone stared at Frances and she started to speak, "This scripture is being fulfilled in front of you." The people at the church were very impressed. But thensome people started to murmur, "Isn't that Mary and Joseph's daughter?" When the murmuring continued, Frances declared, "You will not get to see the mighty works I am capable of. A prophet is never accepted in her hometown. There are oppressed and marginalized people everywhere and you didn't and don't do shit about it. You are a bunch of evil vipers!" The people in the church became enraged. Rushing at Frances, they tossed her out of the church and ran her to the edge of town. Holding her over the side of a bridge as a train rushed by underneath, they would have killed Frances if she hadn't torn free and ran.

Later, Frances went down to the city of Temple and taught there. People were astounded at her teachings. There was a man with a demon and he cried out, "Leave us alone! What business do you have with us Frances of Waco? Have you come to destroy us? I know that you are the Daughter of God." Frances rebuked the demon and said, "Be silent and come out of him." The demon wrestled the man to the ground and came out his eyeballs. Everyone was amazed and said, "What type of woman is able to do such things?" The stories of Frances continued to spread.

After church, Frances entered Simon's house. Simon's mother-in-law was suffering from a high fever and in need of care. Frances stood over here and rebuked the fever. The woman got up and began to feast with them.

As the sun was going down, Frances stood in the driveway and healed every infirmary or sickness brought to him. Demons consistently came out and shouted, "You are the daughter of God!" Frances rebuked them, because she wasn't ready for everyone to know that she was the Messiah yet.

Frances left the church at daybreak and went to a quiet place outside of town to pray. The people found her and begged her not to leave Temple. But Frances said to them, "I must proclaim the good news of the realm of God to other cities as well. This is my purpose." Frances kept proclaiming the message of love in religious spaces throughout Texas.

5.

Surrounded by a large crowd and standing next to a lake, Frances grew increasingly uncomfortable with the pushing and shoving. Spotting two boats, Frances ran and jumped in one. Looking up, Frances saw Petra standing there and asked her to put the boat out a little from shore. Everyone on the shore sat down and Frances started to teach. Once she finished, Frances told Petra to put her fishing nets in the water. Petra replied, "This lake don't have many fish in it. But I will do what you say." Once Petra pulled the net back, fish started jumping in and she was not strong enough to hold it. Signaling for help, others joined Petra and together they brought into the boat a net full of fish. Petra fell down at the feet of Frances and asked her not to look upon her sin. Petra knew that Frances was no ordinary woman. Frances said to Petra, "Do not be afraid. You will follow me and we will save people together." James and John followed too. Once they got to shore, the group left everything and followed Frances.

Frances met a woman covered with leprosy. The woman bowed at her feet and asked to be made well. Frances touched the woman and said, "Be clean." And she ordered the woman to go and give testimony to the largest church in town about what happened. The word about Frances spread and everyone gathered to be healed. She withdrew to deserted places to pray.

Pastors heard the teaching of Frances and could tell that something was different about her ministry. Some men tried to bring a paralyzed man into the building where Frances was. Finding no way to enter, the group lowered the man in from the roof and laid him at the feet of Frances. When she saw their faith, Frances leaned down and said, "Friend, all of your sins are forgiven." The pastors were furious that a woman would claim to have the right to heal people's sins and that she didn't just heal the man outright. Frances could feel that they were upset and said, "Is it better to have your sins forgiven or to walk? So that you might know that I am the Daughter of God, I tell you, 'Stand up and walk.'" Immediately, the paralyzed man got up and started walking. Everyone was filled with amazement and passionately declared, "We have seen strange things today. Glory to God!"

After the healing, Frances saw a brutal police officer named Levi sitting in his squad car and said, "Follow me." The police officer got up, left everything and followed him.

Levi gave a banquet for Frances at his home and there was a large crowd of police officers. There was a large group of people complaining about Frances eating with police officers. "Does she not understand police brutality?" some of the pastors asked. Frances answered, "Those who are sick do not a doctor. I have come to help the sick."

Then the pastors questioned Frances, "John's disciples fast and pray while your disciples eat and drink." Frances replied, "Why would you make people starve and thirst at a wedding? The Daughter of God is here. This is a time of celebration. There will come a time when I am no longer here. That will be the time to fast and pray." She also told them a parable, "No one patches a hole with new fabric. When you wash the garment the fabric will shrink and make the hole worse. No one shakes up a soda to open it. When you open the soda it will explode and spray all over everything in sight."

6.

Frances walked with her disciples through a farm and everyone picked food to eat. The pastors questioned her, "Why are you working on the Sabbath?" Frances replied, "If someone is hungry, they must work on whatever day they can. The Daughter of God is over the Sabbath too."

A few weeks later Frances was teaching at a small church, when a woman with a withered hand approached her. The pastors watched to see if she would interrupt services to heal the woman. Frances knew what they were thinking and said, "Come stand here." The woman walked up and stood there. Then, Frances said to the congregation, "Do you want her to be healed?" After the congregation answered in affirmation, Frances raised her hands and said, "Stretch out your hand."

The woman stretched out a restored hand. The pastors were furious and plotted ways to destroy Frances.

During those days, Frances went up to the mountains to pray. Late one evening, Frances came down and called twelve diverse disciples. Together, the group started to minister to large crowds from all over the wider area. People came to hear Frances' teachings, be healed of their diseases and have their demons removed. Everyone was trying to touch Frances.

Then Frances looked up at her disciples and said: "Blessed are the poor, for the realm of God belongs to them. Blessed are the hungry, for they will be filled. Blessed are those who weep, for laughter is coming. Blessed are you who are hated because of the Daughter of God. The day is coming when everything will be turned around and all will be made right. Woe to the rich, for you have already received your reward. Woe to those who are full, for you will be hungry. Woe to those who are laughing, for you will cry. Woe to those who are spoken well of, for you will experience slander."

"But I say to you that will listen: Love your enemies, do good to those who hate you, bless those who curse you, pray for those who abuse you. If anyone hits you, let them hit you again; and from anyone who takes your coat let them have your shirt too. Give to everyone who begs; and if people steal from you, do not even file a report. Do unto others as you would have them do unto you."

"Anyone can love those that love them. Anyone can do good to those who do good to them. Anyone can lend someone something that they know they will get a reward for. But I tell you: Love your enemies. Do good to those who hate you. God loves everyone. Be merciful with people, just as God is merciful."

"Do not judge. The measure you use to judge will be the same measure applied to you. Condemn and you will be condemned. Forgive and you will be forgiven. Which is a better choice? Give and it will be given to you. Be gracious to people and people will be gracious to you."

"Can the blind guide the blind? Will not both people struggle to know where they are going? Should disciples guide disciples? There is a need for teachers. Why do you point out the speck in the eye of your neighbor when you have a log sticking out of your own? Take the log out of your own eye before you speak! When people start taking their logs out, then and only then will they be able to deal better with their own specks."

"Good trees bear good fruit and bad trees bear bad fruit. Trees are known by their fruit. Good people produce good fruit and evil people produce evil fruit. People are known by their fruit.

Out of the abundance of the heart the mouth speaks and the body acts."

"Why do you call me the Daughter of God and not do what I tell you to do? I will show you what it looks like to come, to hear and to act. When you build your house on a rock foundation the winds or water have difficulty shaking it. Those who build their house right on the ground can expect the wind to blow and waters to flood it in every direction. If you want to have a foundation made of rock, come to me, hear me and act like me. If you reject my teaching and choose to have a weak or no foundation, you can expect for your house to be left in ruin."

7.

After Frances stopped teaching, she journeyed into Mansfield. There was a man with a highly valued worker at his restaurant that was ill and close to death. All of the churches in town prayed for months over the worker to no avail. When the man heard about Frances, he went out to ask her directly if she could heal his worker. When Frances asked why she should do this for him, the man replied, "I love people. I give to charity. I am a good person. I know I am not worthy. Please come to my house?" Frances started walking to the house and turned to the man to question, "If I heal him, are you willing to let the worker join you in the ownership of the restaurant?" With some hesitation, "No matter what it costs, I want to my worker to be healed. You don't have to go any further. Just say the word." Frances replied, "You will have to start seeing him as your coworker. He is healed." The man started to weep and Frances admired how much faith the man had. When the man returned to the house, he found his new fellow owner in good health and embraced him.

Frances then traveled to a town called Stephenville and a large crowd of disciples and seekers followed him. Upon approaching the edge of town, Frances saw a young unarmed dead man riddled with bullets lying on the side of the road. The police shot him. He was his mother's only son and she was a widow; and with her was a large angry crowd from the town. When Frances came across the scene, she had deep compassion. Frances told the mother and widow, "Do not weep." Bending down, Frances told the young man in a loud voice, "Get up!" Immediately, the formerly dead man got up and started to speak. The police sprung into action and moved to arrest the young man. Frances stepped between them and said, "There will be no arrest tonight. Go home and quit shooting people." Fear seized the police officers and they returned home. Everyone that remained glorified God for Frances. Word of what happened spread throughout Texas and the surrounding areas.

The disciples of John could not believe what was going on and reported everything back to John. John summoned two of his disciples and sent them to ask Frances, "Are you the one that we are waiting for or should we wait for another?" Immediately, Frances replied, "Would you be asking this question if I were a man?" John's disciples replied, "We are not sexist." Frances replied, "You are what you are. If I were you, I would work on how you think about women. Now, go and tell John what you have seen and heard: the blind receive sight, the lame walk, the lepers are cleansed, the deaf hear, the dead are raised, the poor have good news brought to them. Don't take offense to any of these actions just because I am a woman. God chooses those the world thinks are weak to shame the strong."

Once John's messengers left, Frances started to talk to the crowd about John: "What did you go out to the desert to look at? A reed shaken back and forth by the wind? What did you go out there to see? Someone dressed in nice clothes? The unafflicted in their fine clothing sit in safe spaces. What then did you go out there to see? A prophet? Yes! I will tell you that John is more than a prophet. This is the man that prophets in the past prophesized about saying, 'I am sending a messenger ahead of my daughter, who will prepare the way for her.' There is no one greater than John, but the first will be last in the realm of God." Everyone who heard these words affirmed them, because they were baptized by John. The pastors who were not baptized by John called the words blasphemy, because they were the real blasphemers.

"What will I compare the people of this generation? What are they like? These folks are like kids who say, 'We played music for you and you refused to dance.' For John the Baptist came eating no bread and drinking no wine and you called him a demon. The Daughter of God has come eating and drinking and you call me a glutton, drunkard and friend of sinners. You folks need to listen to the music of the children and dance."

One of the pastors invited Frances over to her home for dinner. Once Frances took her place at the table, a known sinner came in the back door and brought some nice perfume with her. Weeping, the man started to use the perfume and his tongue to wash her feet and he wiped them with his beard. Without stopping, the man continued to wash and kiss Frances' feet. When the pastor saw this, he freaked out and shouted, "If you are a real prophet then you would not let this continue. You would known what type of sinner this man is!" Frances spoke up, "Listen to me. There was a bank that decided to forgive two debts. One person owed $500,000 and the other owed $5. Which do you think was more grateful?" The pastor answered,

"I suppose the one who was forgiven more." Frances said, "You have answered correctly." Then, turning toward the man, Frances continued, "Do you see this man? I entered your house and you gave me nothing for my feet. This man gave me a full pedicure. I entered your house and you didn't embrace me. This man has not stopped embracing me. You did not give me any type of gift. This man has not stopped. Though his sins are many, they are forgiven. The one who sins greatly is forgiven greatly. The one who sins little is forgiven little." The pastors at the table declared, "Who does this woman think she is to forgive sins?" Frances said to the man, "Go in peace, your faith has made you well."

8.

In town after town and city after city, Frances proclaimed the good news of the realm of God. Amongst the disciples present were Mary Magdalene, from whom Frances cast out seven demons, Joanna, the wife of one of the Governor's top advisors, and Susanna, who consistently provided for the group.

When a great crowd gathered, Frances spoke in a parable: "A farmer tossed out some seeds. Some fell on the pavement and were burned up. Some fell on the dirt road and lived for a little bit. Some fell in the weeds and lasted until the rest of the plants choked it out. Some fell on good soil and grew a hundred fold. Let anyone who has ears to hear listen!"

Then her disciples asked what this parable meant. Frances declared, "You get to know the secrets of God. When I speak in parables, some look but don't perceive and listen without understanding. The seed is the word of God. Only the seed or the word that falls on the good soil and grows is worth anything. Keep your mind and heart like the good soil so that you might grow. Hear the word of God, hold it fast in your heart and bear fruit with patient endurance."

"No one lights a torch and puts it under a bed. You hold up a torch to light the way. Nothing is hidden that will not be disclosed. Nothing is secret that will not become known. Pay attention to how you listen. For those who are good stewards of what they have, more will be given."

Then Frances' mother and brothers came to her, but they could not reach her because of the crowd. And she was told, "Your mother and brothers are standing outside, wanting to see you."

But she said to them, "My mother and brothers are the ones who hear and follow God."

Needing some relaxation on a local recreational lake, Frances got into a houseboat that was owned by one of the disciples. When night came, Frances was asleep in the front of the boat. Early in the morning, the disciples were awoken by a huge tornado heading directly for the houseboat. The boat started to fill with water and was about to flip over. In desperation, the disciples started to scream for Frances, "Save us! Save us! We're going to die!!!" Frances rolled out of her bed and leaned out the window and said, "Stop!" The disciples were amazed that the night immediately turned calm and tranquil. Frances said, "Why did you wake me up? Where is your faith?" The disciples were afraid and amazed, and said to each other, "What type of woman is this, that even the winds, the water and the sky obey her?"

When they arrived on the outskirts of San Antonio, Frances got out of her car and a man with demons came up to her. The man was dirty, homeless and naked. When he saw Frances, he fell down at her feet and shouted, "What do you want from me, Frances, Daughter of God? Please, don't torment me." The demon was afraid of Frances. Then, Frances asked, "What's your name?" The demon said, "Legion. There are many of us." Over and over, the demons begged not to be sent back into the darkness. Frances took pity on the demons and asked them, "Do you want to be saved?" The demons replied, "We are tired of living like this. Can you save us?" Frances replied instantaneously, "Your sins are forgiven." The demons turned into a thousand dazzling angels and flew to heaven to reunite with God. Walking away, Frances blessed a farm with pigs in it.

When folks in town heard what happened, they told anyone who would listen. Everyone knew the possessed man. People came out to see what had happened. When they arrived and saw Frances and the formerly possessed man cheerfully interacting, everyone became afraid. The people who saw it repeated their stories over and over again. Eventually, the leadership of San Antonio asked Frances to leave town. People are often most afraid of that which they can't explain. The formerly possessed man never stopped proclaiming what Frances had done for him.

When Jesus returned to Fort Worth, the crowd welcomed him with great excitement. Everyone was ready to be healed. The pastor of one of the largest churches in town came out. Sabrina bowed at the feet of Frances and begged her to help her dying daughter. As Frances walked to Sabrina's home, the crowds pressed in on her. There was a woman who had suffered hemorrhages for twelve years. No hospital or physician had been able to heal her. The woman came up from behind Frances and softly grabbed at the bottom of her dress. Immediately, the hemorrhaging stopped. Frances asked, "Who touched me?" When all denied it, Petra asked, "Master, the crowds surround you and press in on you." But, Frances said, "I felt the power leave me. I know that someone with faith touched me." When the woman realized that she could not remain in hiding, she started tremble, fell before Frances' feet and said, "It was I." The woman also said why she touched Frances. With awe at the woman's faith, Frances said, "Daughter, your faith has made you well. Go in peace."

While Frances was still speaking, someone came from Sabrina's home and told her that her daughter was dead. Sabrina figured that Frances couldn't help her any longer. When Frances sensed her struggle to believe, she said, "Do not be afraid. Just believe and she will be saved." When they arrived at the house, no one entered the house with Frances except Petra, John and Joan, and the child's parents. Everyone in the house was weeping and wailing. Frances declared, "Do not weep. She is not dead. She is only sleeping." The crowd laughed at Frances. But she took her by the hand and called out, "Child, get up!" Her spirit returned and she was raised. Then, Frances directed her parents to give her something to eat. Sabrina and her partner were astounded, but Frances ordered them to not tell anyone about what happened.

9.

Then Frances called the disciples together and gave them power over all demons and to cure all diseases and he sent them out to proclaim the Queendom of God and to reclaim the world for right. Frances instructed them, "Take nothing for your journey. Whatever house you enter, stay there and leave from there. Whenever someone fails to welcome you, shake the dust of that town off your feet as a testimony against them." All of the disciples departed and went to a variety of towns and places, bringing the good news of God and healing as they went.

The Governor heard about all that was taking place. Some people thought that John the Baptist was raised from the dead. Some thought that Ghandi was raised from the dead. Some thought that John was back. The Governor said, "I executed John. Who is this?" Secretly, the Governor sought to see Frances.

Upon their return, the disciples told Frances the magical things that happened everywhere they went. Together, the disciples and Frances withdrew to a small town called Dublin. A large group of people followed Frances wherever she went and she welcomed them and told them about the realm of God along the way. Frances healed everyone she met.

The day was drawing to a close, and the disciples started to complain about the lack of places to eat and said, "Send the crowds away, so that we can go to a hotel and order some food, this place is deserted." But Frances said to them, "Give everyone rest and something to eat." The disciples replied, "We only have two hamburgers and a few boxes of fries. We can't afford to buy food for all of these people." There were thousands of people present. Frances replied to the disciples, "Get everyone to sit down and start passing out the food." The disciples did as they were told. Everyone ate until they were full and there were multiple huge boxes of food left over. The disciples were in awe.

Frances often prayed alone. Once, a disciple was near her and she asked, "Who do people say that I am?" The disciple answered, "The incarnation of Eleanor Roosevelt or maybe Martin Luther King, Jr." Frances pushed and asked Petra, "Who do you say that I am?" Petra answered, "The Messiah of God."

Frances ordered the gathered disciples to not tell anyone what they just heard and said, "The Daughter of God and humanity must undergo great suffering, and be rejected by everyone, and be killed, and on the third day be raised."

Then Frances said to everyone, "If you want to follow me, you will have to deny your self and take up your burdens and do as I do. Those who try to save their life will lose it. Those who lose their life for my sake will lose it. What does it profit anyone if they gain the whole world and lose who they are? Those who are ashamed of me and my words, I will be ashamed of them in front of my Mother. There are some standing here who will not taste death before they see the Queendom of God."

Eight days after Frances said these things, she took Petra, Jamie and John high up in a tall building. Once they arrived at the top, Frances started to pray. Upon commencing the prayer, Frances' appearance totally changed and she became a dazzling white light. Suddenly, Malala and Ghandi were standing there talking with Frances. The disciples were stunned. The group was talking about all that Frances would accomplish in Fort Worth. Though they were tired, Petra,

Jamie and John stayed awake and refused to close their eyes. Just as the group was leaving, John cried out, "Frances, let us make three altars to worship you, Malala and Ghandi." While John spoke, a cloud came over and overshadowed all of them. The disciples were terrified and fell on the ground. A voice spoke out of the cloud and said, "This is my Daughter...listen to her!" After the voice spoke, Frances was found to be alone. The disciples told no one about what they saw.

After coming down from the top of the building, a great crowd met Frances. Just then someone shouted out from the crowd, "Look at my son! He is my only child. All of a sudden, something happens to him and he falls on the ground convulsing. Your disciples would not help me." Frances replied, "You faithless generation. How long must I sit here with you? Bring the boy here." While he was walking, the boy started convulsing and fell to the ground. Frances placed her hands on the boy and he was healed. Everyone was astounded.

While everyone was very impressed with all that she was doing, Frances said to the disciples, "I will be betrayed by human hands." The disciples didn't get it. Everyone was afraid to ask what the statement meant.

The disciples started to argue about which one was the greatest. Frances heard them and replied, "Whoever loves a child loves me, and whoever welcomes me welcomes the one who sent me. The least among you will always be the greatest."

Jennifer answered, "We saw someone healing people in your name and we tried to stop her, because she was not of our fold." But Frances replied, "Do not stop anyone from healing. Whoever is not against us is for us."

When time started to run out, Frances set her sights on Fort Worth. She sent her messengers on ahead of her. On the way, the disciples stopped in a town outside of Waco. The town was a very misogynistic and patriarchal place. Upon their nasty treatment of Frances and her disciples, Jamie asked, "Do you want us to blow this place up?" Frances turned and rebuked them. The entire group traveled to another town that was much more hospitable.

Late at night along the roadway, someone approached Frances and said, "I will follow you wherever you go." And Frances said to him, "I am not laying my head anywhere." To another Frances said, "Follow me." But the person said, "First, I need to go to a funeral." Frances replied, "Let the dead bury the dead. Now is the time for you to proclaim the Queendom of God!" Another said, "I will follow you after I say goodbye to my friends." Frances replied, "No you should put their hand to the plow and look back."

10.

Frances sent her disciples out in pairs to all the towns of Texas and said to them, "The harvest is plentiful, but the workers are few. May God continue to send you out into the fields. I am sending you as sheep among wolves. Carry nothing. Only accept what is given to you. Be loving and peaceful with all you meet. Heal and feed those who need healing and feeding. Say to everyone, 'The Queendom of God is here!' If a place rejects you, wipe the dust of the place off your feet and move on. God is near to those who take the time to hear."

"Woe to those who refuse to repent. Whoever listens to you listens to me, and whoever rejects you rejects me, and whoever rejects me rejects the one who sent me."

After a few months, the pairs returned and excitedly said, "Frances, we conquered evil and changed the world in your name!" Frances replied, "In my mind, I watched you conquer evil and be who you were created to be. I have given you all authority. Rejoice in the power of God!"

Frances rejoiced in God and kept saying, "Thank you for hiding these things from the wise and revealing them to infants. My mother has granted me all things and I do her will. Anyone who chooses the Daughter chooses the Mother who sent her." Turning to the disciples, Frances said privately, "Blessed are eyes that see and ears that hear! There are many who desired to see and hear what you have seen and heard...but they didn't see or hear."

A lawyer walked up to test Frances and said, "What must I do to inherit eternal life?" She replied, "What do you think?" He answered, "I think I should love God and my neighbor." Frances replied, "Do this and you will live."

But wanting to be justified, the lawyer said, "Who is my neighbor?" Frances replied, "There was a woman who was beaten and robbed on the way from Dallas and left on the side of the road. She was struggling to survive. Someone passed by her from Austin and left her. Someone passed by her from Houston and left her. Someone passed by her from San Antonio and left her. There was a disabled teenager in a wheelchair from Paris who stopped to help her. The young man stayed with her until help came and traveled with her to the hospital. Staying with her until she was well, the two became lifelong friends. Which of these four people was a friend to the woman?" The lawyer replied, "The young man in the wheelchair." Frances replied, "Go and be like him."

Later, the group entered a home in Cleburne where a woman named Martha welcomed Frances and her disciples. Martha had a sister named Mary who sat at the feet of Frances and refused to leave her side. But Martha got frustrated as she was cleaning and preparing the meal and asked, "Frances, do you not care that my sister has left me here to do all this work? Tell her to help me!" Frances replied, "Martha, why don't you get the men to do some of these things? Mary has chosen her spot wisely."

11.

Frances was praying in a certain space, and after she was finished, one of her disciples said to her, "Master, teach us how to pray, as John taught his disciples." Frances said to them, "When you pray, say this: Our Mother, blessed and revered be your name. Your Queendom come. Give us each day our daily bread. And forgive us of our sins, as we forgive those who have sinned against us. Do not bring us into temptation."

And Frances said to them, "Suppose you have a friend and you go to them and ask them for something to eat for you and a friend around midnight. Instead of helping you out, the friend screams at you and tell you to go away. You beg and ultimately your friend comes to the door to give you what you need."

"I am your friend and I will give you what you need without the begging. Ask and it will be given to you, seek and you will find, knock and the door will be open unto you. If a child asked you for food, would you give them a snake? Or if they asked for an egg, would you give them a cockroach? If you would do such things, imagine what our Heavenly Mother would do for those who ask of her!"

Frances cast out a demon of someone who had become mute. Some of the people gathered said, "Francis is the Devil and casts out demons through the Devil!" Frances replied, "How can any good come from the Devil? This woman was healed. How can a house divided against itself stand? The Devil can't be against the Devil and God can't be against God. Whoever is not with me is against me. Whoever does not gather with me is a scatterer."

"When the demon comes out of the person and can find no place to rest, it says, 'I will return to the place I came out of.' When it comes back, the person seems clean. Then it goes and gets a bunch of other demons to join him to raid the body of the person. Ultimately, that person is worse off than they were before."

While Frances was saying this in downtown Dallas, a woman raised her voice and declared, "Blessed is your mamma!" But Frances said, "Blessed are those who hear what I say and follow me!"

When the crowds increased, Frances said, "This generation is evil. Everyone wants a sign. Just believe! The evil that this generation does will rise up and condemn it! A people more evil than the Nazis has arrived. Except, this generation kills through secret and less overt ways."

"No one hides a spotlight. People want to see the light! Besides, a light that powerful would burn whatever covered it. The eyes are the spotlight of the body. Don't let them burn you by doing dumb things with them. Make sure your body is full of light and not burning up because you covered the light with evil."

A public official asked Frances to dine with him. Frances went in and sat down at the table. The public official could not believe Frances did not wash her hands. Frances could tell what he was thinking, "You public officials wash your hands, but the inside of you is dirty as shit. You fools! Don't you know that the one who made the inside also made the outside? Clean your whole person not just your hands!"

"Woe to you public officials. You keep neglecting people for profits. You don't care about the public. You care about feeding your own rotten souls. You love to be seen and heard, but what have you done? You will fall down under the weight of evil and people will trample all over you without realizing it."

Another public official spoke up and said, "Frances, you insult us." To which, Frances immediately replied, "You public officials give people burdens they cannot bear and you don't care. You plunder, loot, kill and destroy in the quiet and secret places of legislative gatherings, business and courtrooms. Woe to you! You destroy those who could save you! You are accomplices to all the crimes of the most despicable oppressors and you will be held accountable. You jail and kill the prophets and apostles. I am not blind to your actions. Woe to you!"

For standing up to them, public officials were generally very hostile to Frances for the rest of her life.

12.

Thousands of people gathered. Frances started to preach, "Beware of the hypocrisy of politicians. Nothing is covered up that will not be uncovered. Nothing is secret that will not be made known. Whatever you have said in the darkness will be heard in the light. What you have whispered behind closed doors will be proclaimed from the rooftops."

"Do not fear those who can only kill the body. Trust in the one who could have destroyed your soul. God forgets no one. Do not be afraid. You are valuable beyond belief."

"Everyone who acknowledges me in public, I will acknowledge before God. Whoever denies me...I will love them until they affirm me. Whoever speaks ill of the Daughter of God, will be forgiven. I will not let you blaspheme the Holy Spirit. The Holy Spirit will tell you what to say in the difficult hours."

Someone in the crowd shouted out, "Can you help me to get my siblings to stop fighting over our inheritance?" Frances said, "How can I be the judge over such a trivial matter?" Then, she turned to the crowd and said, "Life is about more than possessions." Frances then told a parable, "There was a rich man who worked harder and harder to make more and more money. Ultimately, the rich man started to run out of room to put the money he accumulated and he was forced to create financial institutions to put his money into. For years, the rich man worked to build enough institutions to handle his money. The rich man was never able to make enough money or build enough institutions to satisfy him. Those who store up treasures on earth are fools who will never be satisfied. God is all that can satisfy."

"Don't worry. Be Happy. God has got you. Quit striving to get shit. There is nothing about shit that will last. Strive for God. For where your strive is there your heart will be also."

"Be ready and alert to work for love and justice in the world around you. God doesn't want to find you sleeping the revolution of love away."

Petra grew concerned, "Are you telling this parable for us?" Frances responded, "Are you sleeping? I have put you to work. What are you doing for love and justice? Do not let me find you sleeping. If I do, I'm not going to discipline you. I just want you to experience the magic of the march toward justice. For everyone who has been given much, much will be required. Those who are entrusted with much, much will be demanded."

"I have come to set the world on fire. I have a mission. The future is troublesome to me. I did not come to bring peace on earth in the way that you think about it. I have come to divide people so that they might meet a real lasting honest peace beyond the fake peace that everyone keeps talking about."

Frances also told the crowds, "You always listen to the weather forecast. You better listen to my forecast of the present times!"

"Stop suing each other and taking each other to court. Solve your problems amongst your selves. The lawyers and the courts only take your money anyway. Learn to be fair to your opponent."

13.

There were a couple of people present who asked Frances about Hurricane Katrina, "Do you think God allowed the hurricane to hit New Orleans because there was so much sin there?" Frances replied, "That dumbass question is not deserving of a reply."

Frances then gave a short lesson, "Before you cut down a tree, put some fertilizer on it and see if you can get it to grow."

Frances was teaching in one of the congregations in Texarkana. There was a woman who rolled up in a wheelchair. When Frances saw her, she called her over and said, "Woman, you are healed from all your ailments." When Frances touched her, she was already healed. The woman celebrated and cheered.

However, some in the congregation were frustrated because the woman was still in her wheelchair. "Why didn't you give her the ability to walk again?" someone asked. Frances replied, "The sickness was within." Some in the congregation grew angrier, "The woman needs to be made well!" Frances replied, "The woman is more well than you will ever be." The celebration in the congregation drowned out all the haters.

Frances added, "The Realm of God is like the mustard seed that became a great tree. Even the smallest of seeds can bring about the growth of a mighty movement of love."

"The Realm of God is like some basic ingredients that were used to create a delicious cake."

Someone asked Frances, "Will only a few be saved?" To which she replied, "Most people will not be able to make it through the narrow door. I will have to guide you through the fire. The last will be guided first."

One of her friends ran to her and said, "Get out of Texas as quick as possible. The Governor wants to kill you." "Texas! Texas! You have such a thirst for vengeance and blood. Go and tell the Governor that I won't be going anywhere. There will come a time when all knees will bow...even his," Frances replied.

14.

Frances traveled to the home of the pastor of one the big churches in Plano for dinner. Just then, a woman came in to express that her child was stricken with homosexuality and needed to be cured. Frances replied, "You are the one who needs to be cured. Sexuality is something to be celebrated not cured." Lifting her hands, Frances drew the demon of homophobia out of her. The woman was healed. The rest of the pastors present questioned Frances, 'Why did you just do that? Our religious traditions say that homosexuality is a sin." Frances replied, "Your religious traditions are wrong. Do you want me to take away your sexuality?" And they could not reply to this.

When she noticed that everyone was trying to get places of honor at the table, Frances told the gathered, "All who exalt their self will be humbled and the humbled will be exalted." To the ones who planned the dinner, "Stop inviting all these wealthy people to your party! Invite the oppressed and marginalized! Will you not learn more from being with people who are not like you? Open your wallet and your heart."

One of the guests shouted out, "Blessed is the one who will eat in the Realm of God!" Frances replied, "Go ahead and invite all wealthy people to the Realm of God. They won't come. Only those who have been baptized by the love of the marginalized and oppressed in the streets will be able to make it. So get out into the streets and start inviting people! You can't see or move toward the future until you have been with the least."

Large crowds followed Frances and she turned to tell them, "You cannot be my disciple until you are ready to leave everyone and everything. The love of God is all that you need."

"You are the sugar. What good is sugar that does not taste sweet? Sweetless sugar might as well be shit. Let anyone with ears to hear listen!"

15.

The vilest people in all of Texas started hang out with Frances. The pastors and priests could not believe what she was doing, "This woman eats with even the pedophiles and sex offenders!"

Frances replied, "If someone finds redemption, shouldn't you celebrate with them no matter what they've done in the past? If you lost a hundred dollar bill, would you not look for it and be excited when you found it? Are people not more valuable than money?"

"There once was a wealthy man with two daughters. Both daughters asked for their inheritance money early. One daughter used her money to move close by and help to care for her dad. The other daughter used her money to travel the world for many years and try to find her self. Ultimately, the adventurous daughter spent all of her money and went broke in Thailand. Unable to afford a flight back, the daughter called her dad. Glad to hear her voice after all these years, the dad paid for her to come home, said she could live with him and started to plan a party to welcome her back. The daughter who had remained home to care for her dad was furious and demanded, 'Why are you accommodating and celebrating her in such a way?' The dad replied, 'My daughter you are always with me. All that I have is yours. I have not seen your sister in years. We must not miss this opportunity to celebrate. Your sister was dead to us and now she is alive. Your sister was lost but now she is found. Hallelujah!'

16.

Frances kept sharing stories with messages, "Executives usually earn their money on the backs of poor people and don't share their wealth with anyone in need. Don't be like them. Trust those who are faithful to God. You will know the truth when you encounter them. No one can serve both God and money."

The pastors and priests of the wealthy churches grew increasingly frustrated with Frances for saying these things and said, "Our salaries and church buildings come from people with money!" Frances replied, "Maybe you are part of the problem. The temporal stuff that is prized by humans is an abomination to God."

"The Realm of God will not be taken by force. The Realm of God will only be taken by love. God would have to pass away for love to pass away. Love truly endures forever. Those who love will endure in love."

"Be faithful to love. Don't trade love for cheap thrills. Respect marriage and other commitments of love."

"There was a rich man who treated a poor man named Lazarus like shit. When Lazarus died, he was taken up to heaven. When the rich man died, he was kept out of heaven. When the rich man looked up and saw Lazarus in heaven, he begged, 'Have mercy on me! Let me come up there with you!' In his mercy, Lazarus retrieved the rich man and brought him to heaven. Love is stronger than vengeance."

17.

Frances continued, "Don't set up traps of evil for other people. If you trap children, the guilt will make you wish you had never been born. Rebuke disciples that sin and forgive them over and over. If someone keeps committing evil against you, forgive them infinitely."

Under the weight of such statements, the disciples cried out, "Increase our faith!" Frances replied, "If you have the smallest of faith, you will be able to do the biggest of things. Work for God and you will live in the power of God."

On the way to Fort Worth, Frances was traveling through the region of North Texas and entered a small town. Ten people with cancer approached Frances and asked for healing.

Without question, Frances made them well. Only one of the person healed returned to Frances to thank her. Falling on the ground at her feet, the person thanked her over and over. Frances replied, "Where are the other nine?" Then, looking at the person, Frances added, "Get up. Since you came back, you will now be able to go and heal whoever you come in contact with."

Late one day, a group of pastors and priests asked Frances when the Realm of God would arrive. Frances responded, "The Realm of God is already here."

Then, Frances said to her disciples, "The Daughter of God will be like the lightening, here for a moment and gone in a moment. People will endure much suffering and then the Daughter of God will arrive in a flash to usher in the Realm of God. Those who try to make their life secure will lose it. Those who lose their life in pursuit of God will keep it. In my love, I will find everyone and bring them unto me. Then people will ask, 'Where has all of the evil and death gone?' I will tell them to look where the vultures are."

18.

"Pray always and never give up. It gets better. There was a city where violence against minorities was rampant. A local activist refused to stop going to every city official she could think of to demand justice. After a few months, the persistence of the activist convinced city officials to do something about what was going on. Those who committed violence against minorities were punished, children were educated to be more sensitive and inclusive and people started to be good to each other. The world changed. Will not God change your world? Will not God hear the cries of those who call to her day and night? Is there anyone who still has faith?"

"There was a pastor who thought he was God's favorite. Everyday he prayed, 'God, I thank you that I am so much better than everyone else.' There was a worker who worked as hard as he could just to make it. The worker prayed, 'God, help me to be who you created me to be.' The exalted man will never experience the majesty of God with prayers like that. The humble worker is chasing after God's own heart."

While Frances rested in a park, children kept running to him and gathering around them. The disciples tried to chase the kids off, but Frances said, "Let the children come to me, for they are the Realm of God. Whoever does not receive the children, does not receive the Realm of God."

A wealthy young banker asked, "What must I do to live forever?" Frances replied, "Love God and you neighbor." The young banker replied, "I have done that since I was a kid." When Frances heard this, she said, "There is still one thing that you have not done. Sell everything you own and give the money to the poor." When the young banker heard this, he became very sad and walked away.

Those who heard the exchange declared, "Who can be saved?" Frances shot back, "What is impossible for you is not impossible for God."

Then, Petra responded, "We have left everything to follow you!" Frances replied, "Maybe there are things that you still hold on to. Let go and let God."

Frances took her closest disciples to a quiet restaurant and said, "We are going to Fort Worth and I will be killed there. Do not worry. I will rise again." The disciples didn't understand what was being said.

In Flower Mound, there was a blind man standing on the side of the road begging. Someone told him that a group of cars was about to pass and that the religious leader named Frances was in the front car. The blind man shouted out, "Frances please stop and heal me!" Everyone tried to make him quit yelling, but he would not stop. Inside the car, Frances asked the driver to stop and she got out of the car. Approaching the man, Frances kissed the man on the lips and said, "What do you want?" "I want to see," the man replied. Immediately, the man could see. While everyone cheered, Frances got back in the car and drove toward a church in Flower Mound.

19.

Upon arrival at the church, Frances stepped of the car and was greeted by thousands of supporters. There was a local police officer that wanted to see Frances. Being too short to see over the crowd, the officer climbed to the top of the steeple of a church across the street. Frances was about to go into the church where her event was being held. Sensing that there was someone that she needed to see left outside, Frances turned around and looked up to the steeple across the street. Seeing the officer, Frances said, "Officer! I need you to come down from there. I am coming to your house for dinner tonight and need a place to crash." The officer crawled down the steeple quickly. Everyone gathered started to grumble and said, "Doesn't Frances know how evil police officers are? Why would you want to have dinner at the house of one?" Despite the grumbling, the officer looked at Frances and said, "I want to repent of all of the acts of brutality I have ever committed." Frances replied, "Salvation has visited us today! Hallelujah!" After a few moments thought, Frances added, "The Daughter of God has come to seek and save that which is lost not what has already been found."

Going into the church, Frances taught for a few hours. Frances concluded her teaching with a proverb, "Those who have will receive more. Those who don't have will continue to have nothing. Love must be created in order to grow." Upon finishing her teaching, Frances dined and stayed with her disciples at the police officers house.

The next morning, Frances and the disciples left for Fort Worth on public transportation. When they got close to the city limits, Frances asked the bus driver to stop the bus and let everyone get out. Frances told the disciples to go and get a motorcycle for him to ride into town. "How will we pay for it?" the disciples asked. Frances replied, "Tell them God needs it and will bring it back." The disciples found a motorcycle at a small house and the owner gladly handed it over. Placing their coats over the seat to make it more comfortable, the disciples brought the motorcycle to Frances and prepared to enter the city. As she slowly road along, people lined the streets to welcome her and cheer her on. People kept spreading their clothing on the streets for Frances to ride the motorcycle in on. As she pulled up to the middle of the city, all of the disciples cheered and praised God with a loud voice, saying, "Blessed is Frances, the Daughter of God! She comes in the name of God! Peace and glory in the highest of heavens." Some of the pastors and priests in the crowd demanded the disciples tell Frances to make it stop. Overhearing, Frances replied, "If these people don't praise me, the stones would start to cry out."

Frances wept over Fort Worth and said, "Fort Worth! Fort Worth! Do you care about anything more than money? Why do you keep sending people to be executed and call it justice? Do you believe in a God beyond that of your own making? I am here and you have denied me."

When Frances entered the largest church in town, she drove out all the people who were profiting off of God on the backs of the poor and said, "Why have you turned my mother's house into a scam?" Frances started to take back pulpits and demanded that the pastors and priests start preaching about love. The religious and civic authorities teamed up and devised a plan to have Frances killed.

20.

One day, as Frances was sharing the good news of love, a group of pastors and priests demanded of her, "Where do you get the authority to say all of the stuff that you do? Who do you think you are?" Frances replied, "Do you think that Martin Luther King, Jr. was a prophet?" The group of pastors talked for a second and said, "We don't know." Frances pushed back, "If you can't be sure about King, who can you be sure about? I am not interested in wasting any more of my time with you. Your hearts are simply too tightly closed."

"There was a doctor who operated on someone without a license. The person got sick and died. Would you want him operating on you? I wouldn't either. I would want the person who was going to take care of me better than I could take care of my self. Unfortunately, many in this generation have rejected the greatest physician of all. I will heal all that I meet." The words of Frances enraged the gathered pastors and priests. The group wanted to kill Frances, but was afraid of the people who loved her.

Over and over, the pastors and priests kept trying to catch Frances in a hypocritical statement and finally they asked, "Should we pay taxes?" Frances replied, "If the money is made by the government then give it back to the government." Everyone was amazed at the freedom expressed in Frances' answer and the pastors and priests simply could not trap her.

There were a couple of religious people who came up and asked, "If you get married and your wife dies and then you get remarried again, which person will be your wife in heaven?" Frances replied, "What difference will it make? Everyone will be alive in love." The people loved Frances and Frances loved them. Sensing the adoration of the people, no one dared try to trap Frances again.

Then, Frances said to them, "Do you believe the Daughter of God can also be God? How can this be? With God all things are possible."

"The pastors and priests of this generation take from the poor to make the church rich. Such greed and evil can go to straight to hell."

21.

In the midst of a bunch of rich pastors and priests, a homeless widow walked up and placed the money she collected for the day in the offering plate. Frances stood up and said, "This homeless widow has put more in the plate than any of you will ever be able to put in."

"These churches that constantly commit evil are coming down."

"When the world gets so bad that you cannot stand it anymore and everyone gets tired of committing evil, God will change all hearts to love. There will be those who doubt and test that love will win. Do not listen to anyone or anything except God. Make up your mind that love will win and endure in love."

"Fort Worth will not last as it is. Fort Worth will be completely broken down and built back up in love. All will be made well."

"There will be signs that love will win. You will feel it when you practice mercy, grace and generosity to each other. When you feel it, know that I am coming quickly to make all things right and total eternal redemption will come through a massive overwhelming influx of love."

"This generation will not pass away until they have seen and heard these things."

"Be on guard against hate. Practice love. Be on guard against evil. Practice love. We will all stand together in love in the end."

Frances kept preaching and prayed through the night. No one in Fort Worth wanted to miss a single word of Frances' preaching.

22.

The pastors and priests were looking for a way to have Frances killed. One day after seeing Frances show affection to another woman, Julia became enraged and went to tell the District Attorney every lie he needed to hear in order for her to be arrested. Fearful of the crowds, Julia strategized with the pastors, priests and District Attorney about the right time to arrest Frances. The evil plan was under way.

The Great Festival commenced and Frances gathered for dinner with the disciples. A space was magically provided and Petra, Jenna, and John prepared the meal. When the hour to eat arrived, Frances entered the room and said, "I have waited a long time to eat this meal with you. I am about to suffer and die. We will dine again in the Realm of God." Then she took a cup of wine and after giving thanks said, "Take this and drink of it. This is my blood. We will drink it again in the Realm of God." Then she took a loaf of bread and after giving thanks, broke it and said, "This is my body. I give it for you. Take this and eat it. We will eat again in the Realm of God. I do all of this for you. You do this in the future in remembrance of me. The one who is going to betray now holds the cup." Julia left the room.

The disciples started to argue about who Frances loved the best. Everyone wanted to be the greatest in Frances' eyes. Frances replied, "The greatest will be the least and the least the greatest in the Realm of God. All of you will eat and drink with me in the Realm of God."

"Petra, I am praying that you will not fall victim to the evil one." Petra replied, "I will stand by you forever! I will go to jail for you." Frances interjected, "The sun will not rise before you deny me three times."

"Gather your things. We must got to the shore of the Trinity River to pray." When they arrived at the space, Frances looked at the disciples and said, "Pray that you will not falter in this time of trial." Then, Frances withdrew to a solitary place and prayed, "Mother, if there can be any other way...save me from this hour. I will follow you. I will follow you. I will follow you." An angel appeared and gave Frances strength. In her anguish, Frances prayed even more earnestly. Tears of blood fell to the ground. When she got up, Frances found the disciples sleeping and said, "Why are you sleeping? Get up. The hour has come."

While Frances was still speaking, a big crowd came up. Standing in the front, Julia led the group and walked up to kiss Frances on the lips. Before she could get there to kiss her, Frances stopped her and said, "Is this how you are going to betray me?" John screamed out, "What should we do?" Then with little notice, Jenna reached into her pocket, grabbed her gun and shot a Fort Worth Deputy Sheriff. Frances knelt over the Deputy and said, "Stop!" Placing her hands on the Deputy's wounds, Frances healed him. Frances turned to the crowd and said, "Why do you come to arrest me in the night? I have been in public all week and you choose to arrest me under the cover of night? This is the hour of true darkness."

Petra followed the group to the Tarrant County Jail. While she was standing outside, someone approached Petra and accused her of being one of Frances' disciples. Loudly, Petra said, "I don't even know Frances." A little later, an officer pulled Petra over and asked, "Are you with Frances?" "I've never met her," Petra responded. Going back up to the County Jail, Petra was approached again about her connections to Frances and she said, "I just moved here and don't know anyone named

Frances." In that moment, Petra realize she had denied France three times and started to weep.

Throwing insult after insult at here, the police started to beat and torture Frances.

When the morning came, Frances was arraigned before a local judge and charged with terrorism. Prosecutor after prosecutor asked her, "Do you really believe that you're the Daughter of God? Do you really believe that you're the Messiah? Do you know how dangerous it is for all of these people to be following you around? Is this a cult?" "I am who I am. God sent me to save you," Frances replied. The prosecutors and judges had heard enough. "She is an enemy of the state!" everyone in the courtroom cried out.

23.

The Governor was in town and Frances was brought before him the next morning. A large group of pastors and priests were also present. With the pastors and priests blasting accusation after accusation against Frances, the Governor asked, "Do you really expect us to believe that God sent a woman to save us?" Frances replied, "I am who I am." The Governor tried to calm the crowd down and said, "I see no reason to execute this woman." The pastors and priests could not be calmed and said, "If you don't execute Frances, we will make sure that you are run out of office before the year is out for being soft on terrorism and crime."

Once the pastors and priests pushed the Governor sufficiently, he decided to send Frances to the Chief Judge of Tarrant

County. When the Judge saw Frances, she was very glad. "I have been following your work for some time," the Judge told Frances. With the prosecutors, priests and pastors teaming up to hurl question after question, Frances refused to speak. The Judge started to mock Frances and demanded that she answer the questions. When they could get nothing out of her, the Judge had Frances stripped and mockingly put her in a purple robe. Frustrated, the Judge sent Frances back to the Governor. On that day, the Judge and the Governor became inseparable friends.

When Frances arrived, the Governor turned to the crowd with her and said, "You have brought me this woman and called her a terrorist. I do not believe she has committed any crime. I will have her tortured and then released." The prosecutors, priests and pastors got pissed and demanded her execution. The Governor tried to reason with them and no one would listen. There was a mob mentality that had taken hold. The group believed that Frances should die and no one was going to persuade them. One more time, the Governor asked, "What has she done?" The mob screamed, "She is a terrorist and any leader that loves Texas will have her killed!" The Governor turned to Frances and said, "You can stop this." Frances replied, "This is about following God's will not mine." The Governor ordered Frances to be executed.

The prosecutors, priests and pastors led her away and made her carry the rope that they intended to hang her with. There were women standing on the sidewalk screaming out for the execution to stop. Frances to turned to the women and said, "Do not weep for me. I am walking with God. Weep for your self. Weep for this town. Weep for Texas." Two criminals were also being led away for execution. Someone from the crowd yelled out, "You wouldn't be doing this shit if they were white!" The group arrived at a tree next to the Trinity River. Before they strung her up, Frances declared, "Mother, forgive them for they know not what they do." The pastors and priests ripped Frances' clothes off and divided the scraps up. Everyone laughed at Frances as they were about to kick the ladder out from under her. Two criminals were about to be hung on each side of her. People screamed out, "If you are the Daughter of God, save yourself!" There was an inscription placed above her head that read, "The Female God." One of the criminals made fun of Frances and the other believed in her. The generous criminal yelled to Frances, "Remember me in the Realm of God." Frances loved him and said, "I will."

The time was around noon. The pastors and priests kicked the ladders out from under all three criminals. The two criminals died instantly. As Frances hung there for a second between life and death, she said, "Mother, into your hands I commit my spirit." One of the pastors looked on and said, "Frances was innocent and forgave us while we killed her. Maybe she really was the Daughter of God." Even the hardest pastors and priests walked back to their churches and homes wondering if they had made a mistake. Still very afraid, the disciples remained quiet.

One of the pastors was a good man and asked the Governor for the body of Frances. A local funeral home embalmed Frances and she was buried in the church cemetery. Only a few people attended the short memorial service that the pastor held for her. Before she was buried, Petra dropped a love letter on top of the casket and left.

24.

Early on the morning after the burial, a group of disciples went to the tomb of Frances and found the casket dug up and opened. While they were confused, a couple of angels appeared and said, "Do not look for the living amongst the dead. Frances is not here. Frances is risen!" Immediately, the disciples remembered Frances saying that she would rise from the dead. The group of disciples rain back to tell all the other disciples. Jamie, John and the others did not believe them. Petra ran to the tomb and saw the casket open. Amazed, Petra grew more excited with each passing second.

Three disciples were walking from Dallas to Fort Worth in a protest against the death penalty. While they were talking to each other, Frances came up from behind and started talking with them. Not realizing who she was, the disciples started to talk about their pain and heartbreak over the execution of Frances, "We love her. There was no reason for her to be executed. Some people say she has risen from the dead. We find such things difficult to believe." When they got to the end of the protest, the three disciples urged Frances to have dinner with them. After she broke the bread and passed the wine, the disciples recognized Frances and she disappeared. Speaking to one another, they said, "How did we not recognize her? Were our hearts not burning within us?" The disciples ran to the other disciples and told them, "Frances has risen!"

While they were still talking, Frances appeared amongst them and said, "Peace be with you." Everyone in the room was terrified and thought she was a ghost. One even shit in his pants. Sensing their fear and wanting them to realize it was her, Frances invited them to come and feel were the rope was. Everyone touched and knew that it was Frances. While they sat there stunned with joy, Frances asked, "Do you have anything to eat?" Since there was no food in the house, the disciples ordered some pizzas and had them delivered. Later, munching on a slice of pizza, Frances said, "I told you I was God and would never die. You are witnesses of what happened. Feel the power of God come over you. Go and tell the world."

Then, Frances led them back to the Trinity River and lifted her hands. While blessing them, Frances went airborne and went over the skyscrapers. The group watched until they could see Frances no longer. When they were about to walk away, fireworks exploded in the sky and everyone knew that God was celebrating having her daughter back home. The disciples never stopped telling the story about what they saw.

www.ingramcontent.com/pod-product-compliance
Lightning Source LLC
Chambersburg PA
CBHW070512090426
42735CB00012B/2749